Who Me? Worthwhile?
Yes, You!

Who Me? Worthwhile? Yes, You!

A Workbook on Improving Your Self-Image

GLENDA L. HUNTER

RESOURCE *Publications* • Eugene, Oregon

WHO ME? WORTHWHILE? YES, YOU!
A Workbook on Improving Your Self-Image

Copyright © 2009 Glenda L. Hunter. All rights reserved. Except for brief quotations in critical publications or reviews, no part of this book may be reproduced in any manner without prior written permission from the publisher. Write: Permissions, Wipf and Stock Publishers, 199 W. 8th Ave., Suite 3, Eugene, OR 97401.

Resource Publications
An Imprint of Wipf and Stock Publishers
199 W. 8th Ave., Suite 3
Eugene, OR 97401

www.wipfandstock.com

ISBN 13: 978-1-60899-015-3

Manufactured in the U.S.A.

SELF-IMAGE

SURVEYING
  EVERY
    LIVING
      FEELING
        INSIDE
          MYSELF
            AGAINST
              GOD'S
                EVALUATION

CONTENTS

Foreword ix

Acknowledgments xi

Introduction—Where I Came From . . . To Today xiii

1 Who Are You Really? *1*

2 How Do You Really Feel About Who You Are? *8*

3 Am I Angry with Me? *14*

4 What Makes Me Fearful? *21*

5 Can I Really Trust People? *26*

6 Am I a Worthwhile Person? *33*

7 Is There Any Hope for Me? *39*

8 Can I Change My Mindset? *45*

9 Is God in All of This? *51*

10 Who Does God Say You Are? *57*

Summary—Where We Should Be Going 63

Foreword

It is with great pleasure that I write the foreword to this book. The workbook, *Who Me? Worthwhile? Yes, You!* is a powerful and invaluable tool to assist one on the path of inner-self and spiritual awakening, especially in the wake of these turbulent, accelerated times in which we live. Glenda has opened the door to her personal and shared intimacies of her past. A past most of us would care to forget or simply sweep the memories away. These precious jewels of wisdom are to help speed our journey of ascension in consciousness, moving us into greater states of heart-centeredness, forgiveness, compassion and truth.

I physically met Glenda years ago at the clinic where we have worked together. Nevertheless, I continue to be pleasantly surprised by the professionalism she puts into everything she does, be it a program, a counseling session, an article, or an entire book. She is among the few people I know who does not really care how long it takes to complete a task, providing that the result is something she can be proud of and utilize as a tool in transforming lives.

This book goes beyond the excellent writings of an author. As soon as I read the first few pages I was not only surprised, I was overwhelmed with emotion and tears. I could not put it down. I was also anxious to see her the next morning.

As she explains in her introduction, this book is different from most others you can find in bookstores. She has gone beyond what most learned or even know in the area of abuse. She is an amazing woman who has described her life in a few chapters. This is a true memoir about the struggles and successes of a very happy woman. I am proud to have become involved in her life. I have only one caution to the reader. If you are looking for an author who has overcome unbelievable misery and pain to get where she is now, this is the book for you.

She has included at the end of each chapter a practice exercise, a prayer and a meditation. These three practical exercises assist in grounding her teachings in a solid and tangible way. I suggest that you take the time to complete each exercise before moving on to the next chapter. This book serves two purposes, one is to inform you of the effects of a poor self-image, number two is to show you how to be healed and live a healthy and productive life.

Pauline Rogers

Acknowledgments

Thanks to my friends who thought I had a book inside waiting to get out. Thanks to friends who believed in me even when I did not believe in myself. To those that have listened to me question what I was doing, I owe an extra special thank you. Thanks to my proofreader, Ginny; I owe you a new red pen. To the many people who just help me be who I am, I owe a heartfelt appreciation. To my husband, Steve, who has listened to and read all my words, I offer my gratitude.

What is an author but a person who gleans ideas and thoughts from people they come in contact with? Beware, the next time you say something might start a whole story for someone else. So choose your words wisely. Do not be afraid to choose them with humor, as well. Humor helps a weary soul.

Most of all, I thank God for helping me to strive to be the best person I can. Life is not always easy but God makes the difference.

Introduction

Where I Came From ... To Today

By the time I was six, I knew a few things about myself. I was worthless, fat, forgetful, ugly, stupid and would never amount to anything. I started attending church and found them talking about a God that had this strange kind of love. I was intrigued and learned all I could the next few years, but there was something just not right about my life. By fourth grade I had no friends and began to suffer from being suicidal. I never told anyone because I knew that according to God this was not the right thing to do. I didn't have my first Bible until I was fifteen and I read all I could. I guess I was trying to fix what was wrong in my life. I was not even sure what that was. I struggled all the time with self hatred. I even questioned how God could love such a worthless person like me.

I attended Bible College then spent time on the mission field, but I still had a great problem. I could not remember what happened to me as a child, but it affected ever area of my life. I got married. We had two sons. One would think I had everything a person could want. The one thing I did not have was peace of mind. I struggled with the hidden memories of sexual abuse. It was ruling my life. I came across a friend who suggested I get counseling. I agreed but thought it was just another waste of time. Nothing could help the hatred I had for myself and the fear of others that drove me from deep inside. I went without telling my husband, but I had not been going for long when I became suicidal. I didn't want him to know that his wife, the good Christian woman he married, was coming apart. I thought it would be better if I just ended the problem, which was me. I tried to pull out in front of a semi-truck but I just could not get the car to move. I know that was God holding me steady. He had a plan for me.

We were referred to another therapist, who was a Christian, and she informed me I had Multiple Personality Disorder (MPD). Dr. James Friesen writes, "MPD is not a disease. It results from dissociation, a God-given coping style that gifted children learn to use to protect themselves from the effects of traumas." This explained a lot about my life of forgetfulness and my family thought it made sense. Now I have a mental illness. What do I do?

The journey to "better" began. The secret I kept for many years was not an easy one to tell. Every Alter (alternate personality) had to remember, recall, and speak the unspeakable secret. My dad said it was a secret for him and me. If I told, no one would believe me even though I knew I did not lie. I thought he was big, I was little, who would they believe? His threat got bigger as I got bigger. Next he said if I told he would have to leave or they would take me from him and mom. I was sure I didn't want that to happen because then what would I do? When I was six, he must have been concerned that I would tell someone in the church; so with a knife pressed to my throat, he said he would kill me if I told. This was done repeatedly. At any age that would be frightful; but at the age of six, it is really frightful. I lay in bed many a night afraid to go to sleep because of the uncertainty I felt about what might happen in the morning or even while I slept. I tried hard not to fall asleep. When I began to tell my therapist, it didn't matter that my father was dead. I was convinced that he had someone watching and they would get me if I told. My abuse never followed any pattern so who knew if a hug or a hit would happen. My mother knew that something was going on and she didn't stop it, which left me with the feeling that no one would ever care enough to help me. This helped me to be unsure of my therapist and could I tell her my secret? If I did, would we be safe? It took about two years to open up to her. But she was patient and loving. I tried things that tested her. Sometimes I tried to make her mad enough to hit me, but she did not. I did not understand people that did not give up on me. Did she really care about me enough to stick with me in spite of the hard times? She did.

Another fact I found hard to believe: Is this really true? I could not believe this was really *my* family—not my dad and uncles! I did not remember it all these years so certainly it must not be true. This was the kind of thing in other families not mine. Certainly my dad and uncles were not all that bad. This is just a bad dream. I had hoped to wake up from this nightmare any second. But it did not happen. This was not something anyone implanted in my mind: smell, touch, sounds, bright lights, and even dreams triggered the memories. Many of the Alters told the same facts, just a little different situations, sometimes even the same story. This even gave more validity to the memories because the Alters did not share memories. I also had body memories, this is when the body remembers the act and it feels like that moment all over again. I would hurt so bad sometimes I could hardly get around but there was nothing physically wrong. Then I would think, "that's how it felt when" then I knew it was a body memory. I tried hard to continue the denial but it became impossible to deny the facts.

I was convinced it was my fault because that is what my dad told me in a very persuasive way. "You asked for it," were his words. If I weren't such a bad girl, he wouldn't have to do such things. He had to teach me a lesson. I was sure he must be right because he and my uncle weren't bad people, and I already knew I was. I was a preschooler when it started and I wasn't even sure what was going on. But I took all the guilt they wanted to give me. It certainly had to be my fault. It left me with the feeling of being dirty. Just remembering, I would take showers with such hot water I would be beet red when I was done. I also would scrub my body hard, in hopes that the layers of dirt would come off. It did not matter how hard I scrubbed or how hot the water was, it did not help. I struggled with it day and night. I had to work hard at channeling the guilt in the right direction. But with God's help, I was finally able to do that.

Suicide was a constant theme. I never dreamed anyone would even care because I was so much trouble. I called and was talking to a friend one night. While we talked I picked up a pocket knife my husband had on the dresser and began to see how sharp it was. I told her that this knife could never cut anything. I was really trying it on my arm while we spoke. She didn't say much. When we hung up she called right back to talk to my husband and told him what was going on. I never had a clue she even did that until later. But I had told people things like this before and no one seemed to listen. When things got real bad, I always had at least one Alter that would call someone and let them know in someway that there was trouble and checking out was in the making. My therapist tuned her ears to such talk as well. She was always interested to find out if there was a plan. I always seemed to have a plan in the back of my mind if not in the forefront. At one point the knives had to be taken out of the house, even my car keys were taken away. I have also spent my fair share of time in the hospital because I left people with no choice. I'm thankful for people who listened and took action even if at the time I did not appreciate it very much. The Lord gave them ears that really heard what was being said and the courage to do what would not make them popular.

I suffered much pain, at the recall of every memory, not once but many times. I wondered where God was? Did He even know what was going on with me? I figured certainly if He knew the pain I was in, He would help it to stop. The hurting Little One inside wrote this poem:

I HURT INSIDE

God, do You know how I hurt inside?

Do You care that my heart breaks?

I am just a little girl, one that likes to run and play.

I like having a lot of fun.

But I became a sad, quiet little girl when dad began to abuse me.

I was being hurt but no one seemed to care.

I do not know how to tell big people what is going on

But I am afraid they would not believe whatever I said.

My tears are many but they flow on the inside.

I try very hard not to let them slip down my face.

Because when my dad sees these horrible tears he slaps me and becomes very angry.

I am just little but I know what is happening is wrong.

Will this ever end or will I always be afraid?

I often cry and scream on the inside for someone to help or care.

But people walking by have no idea of the hurt that lies deep inside.

God, I do have a big favor to ask You.

Will you please put Your arms around me and hold me close?

I need to be able to rest without fear.

THANK YOU FOR CARING!

I was very ashamed of the secret and wondered how would people look at me now and would God even look in my direction? I was so ashamed of myself. How could I let such a thing happen to me? I had stopped writing letters or calling friends; all I wanted to do was isolate in my house with the curtains closed. I stopped going to church for awhile and was sure that if the church people found out, they would never want me to come through their doors again. I told Steve, my husband, I would understand if he wanted me to leave or if he wanted to leave and take the boys so I would not bring disgrace to the family. He would not hear of that; he continued to be my support. He held me many nights as I cried myself to sleep. I was shocked when I realized that God also was not ashamed of me. With all the great counseling I was getting, I still had to give that to the Lord. When I did, I was able to look myself in the mirror and feel like life was worth living.

Did I have anger? I had a hard time admitting I did. I thought a good Christian should not have anger. Even though I tried to pretend it did not exist, it was still creeping out in all kinds of ways: yelling at the boys, getting angry with my husband over nothing, yelling at my therapist, even being angry with friends for no reason. It was obvious to everyone else that something was wrong. It is very easy to take your anger out on someone else when the truth is too hard to face. Then I read Psalms 7:11; God is a just judge, and God is angry with the wicked every day. Then I began to reason that if God, being the loving God that He is, can be angry with the wicked then I could certainly spend a few days being angry because what happened to me was certainly wicked. I also spent time being angry with God and why he let this happen to me. I was surprised to find out He is big enough to handle it and help me move beyond that point. God was faithful and took that raging anger and replaced it with peace.

God has always given me a desire to be better. I never knew what that meant or how that could even happen but I strived to that end. After hard work, sleepless nights, tunnels that seemed to have no end, I have reached Better. God has helped me to find the wholeness that I was meant to have from the beginning.

WHAT I HAVE LEARNED

I have learned that when family, friends, and counselors are willing to be loving links for hurting people like me, the hard times of life are bearable. When they listen with their hearts as well as with their ears, they will hear those deep cries for help and answer them. They also will be a rescuer or a lighthouse for those drifting in the deep raging sea of life.

I also have learned that God is the great counselor, the great healer, faithful comforter, just judge, God of righteousness, God of wholeness, and a God of true love. Truly He is a loving Father.

1

Who Are You Really?

"The greatest responsibility entrusted to man is that of developing himself."
—William Ross

WHO AM I REALLY? Is this a trick question? No, but it can make you stop and think for a few minutes. It makes me wonder what the person is really asking. Do they just want my name and what titles I hold or do they want my life story? When we think about who we are, many things come into play. Just a few of these things are the way you were raised, the environment, what we were told, who we think people think we are and the list goes on. What I was told about myself was not really true. In believing my families false belief of how I looked and who I was, shaped who I believed myself to be. I believed myself to be a fat, ugly, stupid, worthless no good person and many other untrue things. Is how someone else sees you really who you are? Not always.

So who are you? What lies deep inside your inner being is who you really are. What is that? Sometimes even deep inside, I cannot see the true me. I see what I was told. I was told over and again enough times I believed what was untrue. For many years I have viewed myself as a worthless person who would never amount to anything. Now inside I know that is not true, but it does come back to haunt me from time to time.

I have a wonderful family, a great husband and two terrific sons, who each have wonderful families of their own. I am a good friend, trustworthy, hard worker, caring, and funny, and I can even be serious when times require. Bottom line: I am a good person. That is who I am. Who are you?

1. *Who are you?*

_____

_____

_____

_____

_____

When we think of who we are, many things come into play: the way we were raised, environment, what we were told, who we think people think we are and the list goes on. Is how someone else saw or sees you really who you are?

2. *Do you like who you are? Why or why not?*

_____

_____

_____

_____

_____

3. What do you like the most about yourself?

_____

_____

_____

_____

_____

If you have left these blank then think again and try harder, for your sake.

4. What don't you like about yourself?

> "He who has a big nose thinks everyone speaks of it."
> —Proverb (Scottish)

_____

_____

_____

_____

_____

5. Describe who you are, not what you do.

_____

_____

_____

6. Are you a worthwhile person that someone would be proud to have as a friend? Why or why not?

> "If you were another person,
> would you like to be a friend of yours?"
> —Anonymous

7. Do you think people only pretend to like having you around because they feel sorry for you? Give an example.

8. What makes your worthiness?

_____
_____
_____
_____
_____

Or do you even feel that you are worth anything? Is it your job, your position in the community or a title which you carry that makes you a worthwhile person?

9. What makes you feel the way you do about yourself?

_____
_____
_____
_____
_____

10. Who or what has made you feel this way?

_____
_____
_____

11. Do you think you need to change the way you see yourself? Why or why not?

After taking a good look at yourself, stop and think of who you really are and be honest. If we pretend to be something or someone we are not, we cannot go as far as you are created to go. We cannot accomplish what is meant for us to accomplish. Looking deep inside is a very hard thing to do because sometimes we see things we do not like. But do keep looking; you might be surprised at what you do find.

"Better keep yourself clean and bright;
you are the window through which you see the world."
—George Bernard Shaw

Job was a great man, one who suffered greatly and it would be good to read his words 9:16–35. He had many obstacles to face but he still called on God. Who God was is a question even this great man asked. Do you think you and Job had anything in common? What is he really saying?

PRAYER

Dear God,

Help me see who I am really, not who I pretend to be, but what lies deep inside my being. Help me to come clean with myself so You can fill me more with Your presence and grace. Help me to be honest and truthful in spite of how it might hurt or make me feel. Give me the ability and desire to change those areas I can and courage to stand for what is true and just.

Amen

Now Take a Fresh Look at Yourself as You Ponder Who You Are.

2

How Do You Really Feel About Who You Are?

"Do you know what you look like? Not really."
—Walker Evans

THE BIBLE TELLS US about a group of people, the children of Israel, who were made to serve Pharaoh. But the more they were afflicted, the more they multiplied and grew. The Egyptians made them serve them with vigor. They made their lives bitter and had them do hard labor. They were greatly mistreated but they kept multiplying. They waited for the day when someone would rise up and save them. Moses was that man. After many long years, Moses came to Pharaoh demanding he let the Israelites go, but Pharaoh had a hard heart and refused to let God's people go. Even at the sight of many plagues he kept refusing. The tenth plague when God allowed all of the first born in the entire land of Egypt to die, Pharaoh sent Moses and the children of Israel out of the land. This is when their exodus began.

They wandered in the wilderness and began to wish they were back under the control of Pharaoh. At least there they had three square meals a day and a variety of food. Now all they had was manna, a type of bread. They were not satisfied that God had delivered them from their bondage. They wanted meat and they grumbled until Moses went to God with their request. God said he would give them meat. For three months they had all the quail they could eat. Every morning there was more quail and they died eating what they asked for.

They were not satisfied with what God gave them. They wanted more and nothing seemed to be good enough. They grumbled about every stage of their life. It did not matter how bad or good they had things. They did not really understand who they were.

1. What makes you the way you are?

> "The longest journey is the journey inwards."
> —Dag Hammarskjodd, Makings

_____

_____

_____

_____

_____

_____

2. Do you have to stay the way you are?

_____

_____

_____

_____

_____

_____

3. What would change involve? Can it happen over night?

_____

_____

_____

_____

_____

4. Do you really like who you are? Think long and hard because you only hurt yourself by not telling the truth.

_____

_____

_____

_____

_____

5. If not, why stay there? Or do you have a choice? Everyone has a choice of where they stay. They might not have had a choice where they started, but where they end is truly their choice.

_____

_____

_____

_____

_____

6. What are the two things you would change and why?

> "How slight a change may raise or sink a soul!"
> —Philip James Bailey

_____

_____

_____

_____

_____

_____

7. Now who are you REALLY? Take a good look and peek deep inside.

> "Begin to be and know what you will be hereafter."
> —Saint Jerome

_____

_____

_____

_____

_____

_____

8. What really keeps you stuck in the same old ruts? Shake off the dust and try something new. It is surprising what you might like if you give yourself a chance. Don't let anything rob you of the life that can be yours.

_____
_____
_____
_____
_____

9. Who do you want to be? I don't mean professionally. Look deeper into what makes a person a real person. Now who do you want to be?

_____
_____
_____
_____
_____

> "Let him who would move the world,
> first move himself."
> —Socrates

Read Genesis 1:24–30. How did God create you? What was He thinking? He was thinking thoughts of love and compassion. A person that He could have fellowship with; one made in His likeness. How special we should count ourselves to have such a wonderful Creator. How special we are to Him.

PRAYER

Dear God,

    Let us see what you see in me. Help me to see that you had a reason for creating me. Help me to love and value that one you created. Please help me to open my eyes to the real me and change what I can and better everything else.

Amen

God Does Not Make Junk!

3

Am I Angry with Me?

Anger is one letter away from danger.

ANGER IS A STRONG EMOTION of being greatly upset. Some examples are kicking the dog for no reason, screaming at your husband when he really hasn't done anything wrong or yelling at the children when they are only being children. There are times you are not even sure what the problem is, all you know is that you are angry. I know I have spent many days and nights angry but had no reason why. Now that I have recalled the abuse I suffered, it has released that anger. Sometimes we hide things but they do come out in some fashion. All the shootings and killing we hear of daily in the news is because someone got angry and did not get it under control.

When you are angry at someone for what they have done, who is hurt the most from that experience? You are. Sometimes the person does not even know they have upset you so much. They have said or done their piece and moved on, but you are stuck there at that moment until you release that feeling. The more you think about it, the angrier you become. All kinds of thoughts run through your mind. He should not have done that to me. He has no right to say or do that. He does not even know what I think. He should just mind his own business. When we stay in that situation, it does not allow you to grow and become the person you are supposed to be. You settle for second best. What are you going to do with your anger?

> "It is easy to fly into a passion—anybody can do that—
> but to be angry with the right person to the right extent
> and at the right time and with the right object and in
> the right way—that is not easy, and it is not everyone
> who can do it."
> —Aristotle, *Nicomachean Ethics*, 2.9

1. *Are you angry with yourself? Why?*

_____

_____

_____

_____

_____

2. *What can you do about it?*

> "Things don't change.
> You change your way of looking, that's all."
> —Carlos Castaneda

Change takes a lot of hard work. Are you up to the challenge?

_____

_____

_____

3. What keeps the anger living inside?

> "My life is in the hands of any fool
> who makes me lose my temper."
> —Dr. John Hunter

4. Does it give you a feeling you enjoy? Does it make you feel in control of the situation? Who really is in control?

5. Is the anger because of something you have done? What?
   ANGER: ONE LETTER AWAY FROM DANGER.

   _____
   _____
   _____
   _____
   _____
   _____

6. Is it something that has been done to you? What? We can only move beyond where we are when we look it square in the face and call it what it really is.

   _____
   _____
   _____
   _____
   _____
   _____

7. Is there anything you can do to change either one? How or why?

   > "Christians are supposed not merely to endure change,
   > nor even to profit by it, but to cause it."
   > —Harry Emerson Fosdick

   _____
   _____
   _____

_____

_____

_____

8. If there is nothing you can do to change, then find a positive way to look at your life.

> "Too many things are occurring
> for even a big heart to hold."
> —William Butler Yeats

A positive outlook can do many things and change many things thought unchangeable.

_____

_____

_____

_____

_____

9. Is anger good? When and why?

> "God is a just judge,
> And God is angry with the wicked every day."
> —Psalm 7:11, New King James Version

_____

_____

_____

_____

10. Who suffers the most from anger? Do you think the one holding the anger toward someone is suffering more then the one they hold it against? How does one suffer more?

_____

_____

_____

_____

_____

_____

11. What can you do with the wrong anger? Or are we just to bury it hoping it never rises again?

_____

_____

_____

_____

_____

"The proud man hath no God; the envious man hath no neighbor; the angry man hath not himself."
—Bishop Hall

"In the good man, anger quickly dies."
—Proverb (Latin)

Read Genesis 4: 1–12. What happened when Cain got angry with his brother? When you let anger grow inside, it will come out in some fashion; and as we see from this story, it might not be a very pretty picture in the end. What anger boils inside of you? Examine it and get help fixing it. God had the solution for Cain but he did not listen. Do you want to follow in his footsteps?

PRAYER

Dear God,

    Help me not to let anger take over my being until I explode. Help me to listen and look for the answers you have for me. Lend a hand to me so I am willing to do what you want me to do. Assist me in letting go and being more like you.

Amen
"Be angry, and do not sin":
Do not let the sun go down on your wrath, . . .
—Ephesians 4:26

4

What Makes Me Fearful?

"The greatest fear comes when God is a stranger..."
—Billy Graham

THERE ARE MANY THINGS that make us fearful, like the dark, heights, losing a mate, and losing a job. I challenge you to stop for a moment and think about what makes you fearful. Some of the things that make me fearful are losing my mate, having something happen to my children or grandchildren, losing my job, people not liking me and the beat goes on. Sometimes I can be a very fearful person. But the trick is not to let it rule your life.

I have always felt like I was not good enough for anything. Therefore, everything I tried I did in fear. I was afraid that if people really found out who I was they certainly would not like me. Everything I worked for would be over. Being fearful can cause you to always be looking over your shoulder wondering what was going to happen next. You become afraid that something bad was waiting down the line for you, therefore, you chose to stand still. When fear controls you, you do not move far or at all. Let God help you get over the fears that cause you to shudder whenever you think of facing the world. The world can be a scary enough place without carrying added, unnecessary fear. What will you do with your fear? I have chosen. Let God handle those kinds of fears in my life. It is not always easy but worth the effort.

1. *Does fear have a big hold on you? How?*

_____

_____

_____

_____

_____

2. *Am I fearful because of what people think or what I think they think of me?*

> *"The fear of man brings snare,*
> *but whoever trusts in the Lord shall be safe."*
> *—Proverbs 29:25 (New King James Version)*

_____

_____

_____

_____

_____

_____

3. *Am I afraid people would no longer like me if they really found out who I am?*

_____

_____

_____

_____

_____

_____

4. *Am I afraid I will never measure up? Why and to whom?*

_____

_____

_____

_____

_____

_____

5. *By whose ruler are you using to measure yourself? Sometimes people use different measuring sticks: you must find the one God uses then see how you measure up.*

_____

_____

_____

_____

_____

_____

6. Am I afraid I am not good enough? Why?

7. Who do you think you are not good enough for? Does that person really matter that much? Why?

8. How good does a person have to be to be good enough?

9. When will you be good enough or will you ever?

_____

_____

_____

_____

_____

> "You gain strength, courage and confidence by every experience in which you really stop to look fear in the face. You are able to say to yourself, 'I lived through this horror. I can take the next thing that comes along, . . .' You must do the thing you think you cannot do."
> —Eleanor Roosevelt

> "It is alright to have butterflies in your stomach. Just get them to fly in formation."
> —Dr. Rob Gilbert

Read Psalm 139: 13–18 God has always known you and has loved you from the beginning. We should not let people make us feel any less worthy than He has created us to be.

PRAYER

Dear God,

I count it a privilege to be counted among one of your creations. Rally round me with your fearlessness to enable me that great feeling. Abide in my every being so the fears will be chased away. Give me your peace in all things.

Amen

> "... I am fearfully and wonderfully made; marvelous are Your works..."
> —Psalm 139:14 New King James Version

5

Can I Really Trust People?

"The willingness to trust others even when you
know you may be taken advantage of is the
cornerstone of becoming civilized."
—O. A. Battista

Trust, according to webster, is "to place confidence in" and he also says confidence is "the quality or state of being certain." When a person has done something to you, it breaks all the trust you had for them. It forms questions of certainty you had for other people even when that person gives you no reason to question. Once you feel betrayed it is hard to trust again.

I grew up in a situation that did not teach trust. I was always afraid of people and wondered what they wanted from me. I never knew from one minute until the next what was going to happen. I could not imagine a person just wanting to spend time with me because of who I was. What did cross my mind was what do they want from me and what is it going to cost. I could not think of people as being trustworthy. I had been hurt and I needed to be on guard all the time so no one would hurt me. I was afraid of being hurt again if I put down my guard. For me to trust someone it had to be earned.

I did not know this quote then: "When we trust our brother, whom we have seen, we are learning to trust God, whom we have not seen" by James Freeman Clarke. Needless to say I had trouble trusting God. I never understood how loving and forgiving He can be. This was very foreign to me and my way of thinking. But when I am able to see Him in this light, it is easier to trust in Him. I challenge you to look at God in a different way if you have the same problem I did.

1. Do you have a hard time trusting people? Why or why not?

_____

_____

_____

_____

_____

_____

2. Do you feel like you might be betrayed when you reach out to another person?

_____

_____

_____

_____

_____

_____

3. Can you be trusted when someone reaches out to you? Or do you try to sabotage a relationship before the other person has the opportunity to hurt you?

_____

_____

_____

_____

4. Have you been betrayed when reaching out? Do you still harbor that hurt?

> "... When we are hurt it is important to remember that God Himself has allowed it for a purpose."
> —Billy Graham

_____

_____

_____

_____

_____

5. How do you handle rejection?

> "We ought not to keep score of the number of times others have hurt us, God keeps records, and vengeance belongs to Him."
> —Lehman Strauss

_____
_____
_____
_____
_____
_____

6. Do people say one thing about trust and mean something different? Have you ever betrayed someone's trust? For example:

_____
_____
_____
_____
_____
_____
_____

7. Have you ever found anyone trustworthy? Who and what made them different?

_____
_____
_____
_____
_____
_____

8. How can someone gain your trust or can it ever happen?

_____
_____
_____
_____
_____
_____

"Trust men and they will be true to you: treat them greatly, and they will show themselves great."
—Ralph Waldo Emerson

9. Do you have a friend that has gained your trust? What is this person like?

> "It is better to suffer wrong than to do it,
> and happier to be cheated than to trust."
> —Samuel Johnson

_____

_____

_____

_____

_____

_____

10. ARE YOU TRUSTWORTY? HOW DO YOU KNOW?

> "We are here to add what we can <u>to</u>,
> not to get what we can <u>from</u> life."
> —Sir William Osler

_____

_____

_____

_____

_____

_____

> "You may be deceived if you trust too much, but you
> will live in torment if you do not trust enough."
> —Frank Crane

> "The world is now too dangerous for anything but the
> truth, too small for anything but brotherhood."
> —Arthur Powell Davies

Read 1 Samuel 20. David and Jonathan had a great friendship which was stronger then blood. 2 Samuel 9 tells that David restored to Jonathan's son, Mephibosheth, greatness, but it was nothing he had earned. It was given because of the covenant David had with his friend Jonathan. We should not only grant people things that we feel they have earned, but grant them the greatest of all, respect and trust. Giving of ourselves is the only gift some people are ever looking for.

PRAYER

Dear God,

Help me to treat others as you would have them treat me. Knowing that we are not perfect but by your grace we are saved. Assist me in loving others with all their warts and wrinkles, because we all have problems. Let me give to others some of myself that all will be enriched by your greatness.

Amen

> "Trust in the Lord with all your heart, and lean not on
> your own understanding: In all your ways acknowledge
> Him, and He shall direct your paths."
> —Proverbs 3:5–6 (New King James Version)

6

Am I a Worthwhile Person?

(The Lost Son) "... I am no longer worthy to be called
your son. Make me like one of your hired servants."
—Luke 15:19 (New King James Version)

AM I WORTHWHILE? BRINGS TO MIND a story in the Bible, Luke 15:11–24, commonly known as the story of the prodigal son. The younger son went to his father and said, "Give me what is mine." The father did and the son left. The son left home and lived a wasteful life. He spent all he had and could only find a job feeding pigs. He also ate the food that he fed the pigs because no one would feed him. This was a very lowly job and he began to dream of home. The servants have it better off than I do. He was sure his father would not take him back. What have I done? What am I going to do? I have been very thoughtless of my father. I have brought disgrace to the family name. I am not even worthy to be called his son anymore. But maybe my father will have pity on me and let me serve him as a slave. I will not ask for anything from him if he will only take me back. With his head down in shame, he started his long walk home.

His father was not angry. He was pleased to know that his son was back. He had worried about the health and welfare of his lost son. His joy was beyond measure. He gave a big party in honor of him. He gave him the best he had. He thought he was worthy enough to be called his son again. He had not given up on his young son.

We all have done things in our lives that make us feel unworthy. But God counts us as worthy. Should we count our worth on what people say or God?

1. *What makes you question your worthiness? Is it things you have or have not done? Or is it the family you grew up in? Just what puts this question in your mind?*

_____

_____

_____

_____

_____

_____

2. *What would make a person more worthy?*

_____

_____

_____

_____

_____

_____

3. How do you measure your worthiness?

_____
_____
_____
_____
_____
_____

4. What do others think of your worth? What do they say about you?

> "Therefore do not fear;
> you are of more value than many sparrows."
> —Matthew 10:31 (New American Standard Version)

_____
_____
_____
_____
_____
_____

5. Do you listen and value other's opinions of who they say you are? Why or why not? Then what do you do with that information?

_____
_____
_____

6. Do you listen to their opinion or question them because you feel they are only trying to make you feel good about yourself? Do you wonder what they say behind your back? Do you think it would be the same?

7. What do you really think of yourself? HONESTLY!

> "What lies behind us or before us are tiny matters compared with what lies in us."
> —Anonymous

8. *How can you change a bad view of who you are? Or is there any hope in change?*

> "Love not what you are but what you may become."
> —Miguel de Cervantes

_____

_____

_____

_____

_____

_____

9. *How do you learn to value yourself?*

> "The greatest responsibility entrusted to man
> is that of developing himself."
> —William Ross

_____

_____

_____

_____

_____

_____

10. *What is your true value? Jesus stretched out his arms and gave His life for you (Matthew 27:50). That should let you know how valuable your life is to Him.*

> "Look at the birds of the air, for they neither sow nor reap nor gather into barns; yet your heavenly Father feeds them. Are you not of more value than they?"
> —Matthew 6:26 (New King James Version)

_____

_____

_____

_____

_____

_____

Read Luke 23-24, Jesus gave His life for you, that shows great value. He did nothing wrong, even Pilate said he found no fault in him but he gave Jesus to the angry crowd and they crucified him just the same. Write this scripture again with His love for you in mind. Now ask yourself how valuable you are.

PRAYER

Dear God,

    Please let me see the value you do in my own life. Sometimes my eyes are closed to what you really have made. Enlighten me.

Amen

Being worthwhile is only what we place on it; if we feel worthless, then that is how we will act. If we allow God to fill us with His worthiness, then we will be worth more than we can ever imagine. This is not always in man's sight but in God's where it really counts.

7

Is There Any Hope for Me?

"When you say a situation or a person is hopeless,
you are slamming the door in the face of God."
—Charles A. Allen

IN JOHN 4:1–38, Jesus talks to a Samaritan woman. It was unheard of for a Jew to have anything to do with a Samaritan in the first place, let alone take time to really talk to them. But here Jesus is at the well having a conversation with the Samaritan woman. He tells her about living water. She wanted this living water He told her about. He told her to go get her husband. This opened a can of worms. She had five husbands and the man she now lived with was not her husband. Jesus already knew this and His knowledge of her situation astounded her. Jesus did not find her to be a hopeless case. He continued to talk to her and explain about worshiping God in spirit and truth. The disciples came and wondered why He would be talking to such a woman.

The lady dropped her water pot and ran back into town. She was so shocked that Jesus knew all about her that she told all the men. Jesus did not give up hope for this lady even though her past was not that of one He would promote. He helped her to see the light. The men she went back to talk to also knew her. They probably wanted to see if what she said was really true. They also went out to see and listen to Jesus. They asked Jesus to stay with them and He did for two days. Many more believed because of His words. Had Jesus given up on this woman, many people would not have been touched or received Him.

Jesus does not find us as hopeless cases. Sometimes men see us that way but we mostly look beyond what they say. What really counts is what does Jesus say!!

1. *For a worthless person like me, is there truly any hope? Why or why not?*

_____

_____

_____

_____

_____

_____

2. *Am I worth others having concern for me? Why or Why not? God thought so. He did give His son for you.*

_____

_____

_____

_____

_____

_____

3. Can I really believe there is hope for me?

> "There is no medicine like hope, no incentive so great, and no tonic so powerful as expectation of something better tomorrow."
> —G .K. Chesterton

_____
_____
_____
_____
_____

4. What can I do to earn hope or do I have to earn it?

_____
_____
_____
_____
_____

5. What can I do to gain the hope that is waiting for me? Accept Jesus Christ as your Savior, because He alone is your hope.

_____
_____
_____

_____

_____

_____

6. Is hope only as good as our works? Why or why not?

_____

_____

_____

_____

_____

How sad this would be if that is really true because our works aren't always very good. We are human and we are not perfect no matter how hard we try.

7. If I stumble and fall does my hope go down the drain with my failure? What is your hope made from?

> "Hope is itself a species of happiness, and perhaps,
> the chief happiness which this world affords."
> —Samuel Johnson.

Everyone deserves to be happy, so hang onto that happiness of hope, all of your days.

_____

_____

_____

_____

_____

_____

8. How do I pull myself up again and dust myself off to press on?

> "Someday all you will have to light your way will be a
> single ray of hope and that will be enough."
> —Kobi Yamada

_____

_____

_____

_____

_____

_____

9. What is hope really to me?

> "For Thou art my hope; O Lord God,
> Thou art my confidence from my youth."
> —Psalm 71:5 (New American Standard Version)

_____

_____

_____

_____

_____

_____

_____

10. How can I keep this HOPE?

_____

_____

_____

_____

_____

> "Now faith is the substance of things hoped for,
> the evidence of things not seen."
> —Hebrews 11:1 (New King James Version)

Read about Job's three friends (Job 4–26). How they could have filled him with hopelessness but Job stands firm in what he believes about himself (Job 27–28). It is good to have friends, but do not let them be the downfall of your worth in the sight of the Lord. He does value you more then you can imagine.

PRAYER

Dear God,

Grant to me the hope you have to pick me up when I stumble and brush me off giving me a new start. Let me not lose hope no matter what the situation happens to be or holds for me.

Amen

> "Therefore my heart is glad, and my glory rejoices; my
> flesh also will rest in hope."
> —Psalm 16:9 (New King James Version)

8

Can I Change My Mindset?

"Christians are supposed not merely to endure change,
nor even to profit by it, but to cause it."
—Harry Emerson Fosdick

CHANGING YOUR MIND IS an easy thing to do, it takes just a matter of minutes. But changing your MINDSET is more difficult. Your mindset is the whole way you think. This is something you spend your whole life doing, learning how to think. If you are told something over a number of times, you start to believe it as fact. It does not matter if it is true or not. Your mind gets set in that way of thinking. You tell a child something negative about who they are and they will grow up to believe it is true. To change negative information to positive is a thing that can take many months or even years. There are some steps you have to follow to make that happen. First, you have to be told by someone you trust that it is incorrect. Second, you have to believe the new information. Third, you have to receive it into your thinking. Fourth, you have to say to yourself it is true. Lastly, you have to truly believe the positive. Sometimes that takes daily telling yourself you are a good person and worth something. It is not an easy process but a doable one. Do not let the negative words of your past and possibly of your present dictate how you view yourself. Make it a real effort to dwell on the positive things you know about who you really are. "All the water in the world cannot drown you- unless it gets inside you." (Mary Manin Boggs) It is the same with negative thinking.

> "A man is not finished when he's defeated:
> he's finished when he quits."
> —Richard Nixon

1. Suppose I have always been told bad things about myself. Is there a way that can be changed? Write down bad things that were said, then replace them with good and positive things.

_____

_____

_____

_____

_____

2. What we think we are, that is what we become. What do you think of yourself?

> "Thought once awakened does not again slumber."
> —Thomas Carlyle

_____

_____

_____

_____

_____

3. What are positive things about yourself? Begin by making a list of encouraging things you might have heard someone say about you, then branch out into your own thoughts.

_____

_____

_____

_____

_____

_____

4. List people who say encouraging things about you and choose to make them your good friends. Think of people who fit that description and dwell on those people and what they say even if you think it is not all true. Most likely it is truer than you think.

_____

_____

_____

_____

_____

_____

_____

5. Write uplifting things that you can go back to and read whenever the negative ideas pop back into your head. After awhile they should just become a part of you and you will not need to read them anymore because they will be in your head already.

_____

_____

_____

_____

_____

6. Do you deserve to feel pleasure deep in your being? YES!

> "Make not your thought your prison."
> —Anonymous.

Why do you deserve to feel good about yourself?

_____

_____

_____

_____

_____

_____

7. Keep thinking of yourself in light of the facts you have already written down. Take a few minutes to write even more that might come to your mind now.

_____

_____

_____

_____

_____

8. Do positive self talk. No, I do not mean to go around all day talking to yourself out loud because then someone might think you have gone crazy. I mean in your mind, tell yourself things that will build your image instead of putting yourself down.

_____

_____

_____

_____

_____

_____

"First doubt, then inquire, then discover.
This has been the process with all our great thinkers."
—H. T. Buckle

Read Psalm 27. Desire to do these things and one will have the right thinking and attitude about who God really is and how precious we are in His sight.

PRAYER

Dear God,

    Grant to me the right way to think about Your creation, me. Give me the desire to come and dwell with the one that has made me special and has kept me from the wicked one.

Amen

> "Change favors the prepared mind."
> —Louis Pasteur, speech, 1854

9

Is God in All of This?

"Before I formed you in the womb I knew you;
before you were born I consecrated you;
I have appointed you a prophet to the nations."
—Jeremiah 1:5

SOMETIMES I LOOK AT my life and wonder is God in all of this? I question how could He ever let this happen to me? Why is this the life I was dealt? Where is God in all of this anyway? Is God in all of this? You might feel that He formed you in your mother's womb then forgot about you. He has not. Your life was planned out by Him. What messes it up is the free will He gave us. Sometimes we make unwise choices. This is you stepping out of what He has for you. It does not mean He is leaving you. He is waiting on you to see the light and come back to Him. Other times other people make unwise choices that affect your life. He gives you the grace to handle it. Yes, it causes problems but He is still watching over you. He keeps you in His hand waiting for you to see Him. It might take a long time for you to see that He really loves you. You might make wrong choices because of the anger and hurt you are experiencing. You also might be angry at God for allowing these things to happen. That is okay; He is a big enough God to handle all your feelings. Remember He gave them to you. He has a purpose in all things good and bad. Remember He is there waiting with outstretched arms for you to look in His direction. He will help you to make good out of the bad that you suffered.

> "Every noble work at first is impossible."
> —Carlyle

1. *Of course, God is in this entire situation where you least expect Him. He is in the very words and acts which happen to encourage you everyday. Write down something encouraging that happened to you today. Now think about how God was in the situation.*

_____

_____

_____

_____

_____

2. *God has His hand in our past also. It does not matter how hard or easy it was. What matters is what are you going to make of your state of affairs? Will you allow your past always to dictate what you do from this moment forward or will you permit God to lead and direct your path?*

> "No one can ever wrong you
> as much as you have wronged God."
> —Lehman Strauss

_____

_____

_____

3. *Think of the great people in your life; write down why you think they are great. If you can think of no one, then write what you would look for in a person you would consider great. God will bring them to you if you just stop running long enough to see them.*

_____

_____

_____

_____

_____

4. *He is in the beauty of the day. He has given us a day to live; how we live it is up to us. We can choose to see only blackness or we can see the light. What do you choose and why?*

_____

_____

_____

_____

_____

5. Keep your eyes and ears open today and write the ways in which you see God? Look for the good in those around you and the beauty of His creation. If you still do not see any, ask God to open your eyes that you might see and your ears that you might hear those things He has for you. It might surprise you what you find in your day.

_____

_____

_____

_____

_____

_____

6. He does love you!! Write how that statement makes you feel.

_____

_____

_____

_____

_____

_____

7. *Think about the fact that He gave His ONE AND ONLY SON for your sins. How does that make you feel?*

> "When the Lord does it, He does a thorough job."
> —Corrie ten Boom in Pamela Rosewee's,
> *The Five Silent Years of Corrie ten Boom*

_____

_____

_____

_____

_____

_____

8. *Now do you think God is in all of this? How?*

_____

_____

_____

_____

_____

> "God could have kept Daniel out of the lion's den . . .
> But God has never promised to keep us out of hard
> places . . . What He promised is to go with us through
> every hard place, and bring us through victoriously."
> —Merv Rosell

Read Psalm 91. God can be our protector but we do have to choose to let Him. We can tie His hands by not letting Him do what He so longs to do for us or we can untie His nail-scarred hands and let Him protect us the way He would like to. Life is not always easy but God is always there around every corner.

PRAYER

Dear God,

Allow me to come to you in all my brokenness so you can fix me as good as new. Open my eyes that I might see you, open my ears that I might hear you, and open my heart that I might feel you.

Amen

"By humble experience man has learned that there are very few things in this world worth getting upset about. He knows that if he does his best, God will do the rest."
—John Miller

10

Who Does God Say You Are?

*"You specialize in something until one day
it is specializing in you."*
—Arthur Miller

GOD SAYS WE ARE HIS CHILDREN. He made us. He first made Adam out of dust then He made Eve from his rib. He made us out of His own image. Just think about how awesome that really is. The Bible does not say that He made anything else out of His image, just mankind. That makes us very special. There is no better image to be made after. Would you like to be made in the image of some animal? I would not, as cool as some of them are, I would not like to be made in their image.

God has given us the Bible in which He talks to us. Every day we can read something and learn a new truth. It tells how much He loves us. In it He gives us guidelines on how to live our lives. He also tells us how to treat each other. In it there are godly men and women who have laid the groundwork for our walk with God. But you also find how people struggled. Some did not turn back to God and they were doomed. Others turned their hearts back to God and enjoyed the victory He gave them.

The Bible is full of many helpful things and examples. But I think the greatest is how He has created us to have a free will. This shows to me how much he really loves us. He gives us choices in our lives. I cannot fully comprehend how great that love really is but I do know that He has created us all with a plan in mind. Being in His image tells me that is the case. We each have a purpose. Some of us might have to look a little harder then others but it is there waiting for us to claim it. God has made you who you are for a reason. What might it be?

1. *We are the apple of His eye. What does that mean to you? When I hear this I think of my children and grandchildren. I adore them and would do anything for them. I look upon them with great admiration waiting to see what things they will do or what they will become. They give me pleasure because they are who they are.*

_____

_____

_____

_____

_____

2. *Do you think He is into rotten apples? Take a few minutes and think about what that says about you. How does He see you?*

"You are a child of God. Please call home."
—Anonymous

_____

_____

_____

_____

_____

3. Does He make junk? *I look around every day and see the marvelous things He has created and I do not see junk. I see things of great value and beauty.*

> "Beauty is a gift from God."
> —Aristotle

_____

_____

_____

_____

_____

_____

4. *The Scripture says we are His children.*

> "... And all of you are children of the Most High."
> —Psalm 82:6.

Describe what kind of father you think God is to you, keeping in mind His great love for His creation.

_____

_____

_____

_____

_____

_____

5. We are made in His image (Genesis 1:6). Just what does "in His image" mean to you?

_____

_____

_____

_____

_____

6. 1 John 3:1–2, "Behold what matter of love the Father has bestowed on us, that we should be called the children of God! Therefore the world does not know us, because it did not know Him. Beloved, now we are children of God; and it has not yet been revealed what we shall be, but we know that when He is revealed, we shall be like Him, for we shall see Him as He is." (New King James Version) What do these verses say to you?

_____

_____

_____

_____

_____

7. Describe what God is like?

> "Sometimes the Lord calms the storm;
> sometimes He lets the storm rage and calms His child."
> —Anonymous

_____

_____

_____

_____

_____

_____

8. NOW WHO ARE YOU THAT WE SHOULD DISLIKE HIS CREATION?

> "God only expects one thing of you: that you come out of yourself as far as you are a created being, and let God be God within you."
> —Meister Eckhart

_____

_____

_____

_____

_____

_____

> "... With men it is impossible, but not with God;
> for with God all things are possible."
> —John 1:1 (King James Version)

WHO ME? WORTHWHILE? YES, YOU!

> "God does not ask about our ability or our inability,
> but our availability."
> —Anonymous

Read Matthew 19: 13–30. We are God's children if we are born again into His family. All He asks of us is that we do His will. What is His will for you? This is the question you need to ask yourself. Listen for the answer He gives you. Then get busy about Your Father's business. We all have road blocks in our way from time to time but it is our responsibility to climb over them and keep on going. The going might get slow for awhile but keep hanging in there and do the best you can. That is what He is asking of you.

PRAYER

Dear God,

Thank you for being a loving Father to me. Help me to keep my eyes turned upon You. Allow me to keep in mind that I am created in Your image, therefore, I need to act pleasing to You, our Father. May I always love You as deeply as You love me.

Amen

> "God bless us every one."
> —Charles Dickens

Summary

Where We Should Be Going

> "Even if we may not always understand why God allows certain things to happen to us, we can know He is able to bring good out of evil, and triumph out of suffering."
> —Billy Graham

THIS WORKBOOK IS NOT a guarantee for the best self-image in the world, but one thing I trust it has done for you is help you start on the right track. It is the groundwork to a better you. Be honest and open (even if it is only with yourself) with what is inside then change what you can and sharpen what you cannot.

> "God, give us the grace to accept with serenity the things
> that cannot be changed;
> Give us the courage to change the things
> which should be changed;
> Give us the wisdom to distinguish
> the one from the other."
> —Reinhold Niebuhr, often called the 'Serenity Prayer'

God has a plan for your life. What you do with that is totally up to you. But if you harbor hatred, resentment, and bad feelings towards others, it will only hurt you in the end. We must forgive and move on to bigger and better things.

We all want to be better people than those who have mistreated us. But we must remember that even in that mistreatment, God has a plan. It is hard to see just what He has when we hurt deeply. We need to put all that aside and look toward bettering ourselves. Keep in mind always that God created us for His pleasure not for others. When we try to earn someone else's pleasure, we are only selling ourselves short of what is really in store for us. "Many a man thinks he is buying pleasure, when he is really selling himself a slave to it." —Benjamin Franklin. Do you want to be a slave to others or unconditionally loved by God? That is a no brainer. Unconditional love is what our hearts long for. We cry out for the kind of love that will look at us with all our wrinkles, warts, and ugliness and still care about who and what we are. God can and does do that very thing.

Read back over the things we have discussed when you think that you are no good and not fit to be around. If you never have those times again, then great for you. But some of us will again visit that place of worthlessness; however, the key is not to stay there, but to leave as soon as possible.

It is never too late for a fresh start!!!

EMERGENCY TELEPHONE NUMBERS
(THESE ARE MORE EFFECTIVE THAN 911)

I want to include a list of emergency telephone numbers that I received by way of an email. I think they might be of great help to you in future days.

When—

You are sad, phone John 14

You have sinned, phone Psalm 51

You are facing danger, phone Psalm 91

People have failed you, phone Psalm 27

It feels as though God is far from you, phone Psalm 139

Your faith needs stimulation, phone Hebrews 11

You are alone and scared, phone Psalm 23

You are worried, phone Matthew 8:19–34

You are hurt and critical, phone 1 Corinthians 13

You wonder about Christianity, phone 2 Corinthians 5:15–18

You feel like an outcast, phone Romans 8:31–39

You are seeking peace, phone Matthew 11:25–30

It feels as if the world is bigger than God, phone Psalm 90

You need Christ-like insurance, phone Romans 8:1–30

You are leaving home for a trip, phone Psalm 121

You are praying for yourself, phone Psalm 87

You require courage for a task, phone Joshua 1

Inflation and investments are hogging your thoughts, phone Mark 10:17–31

You are depressed, phone Psalm 27

Your bank account is empty, phone Psalm 37

You lose faith in mankind, phone 1 Corinthians 13

It looks like people are unfriendly, phone John 15

You are losing hope, phone Psalm 126

You feel the world is small compared to you, Psalm 19

You want to carry fruit, phone John 15

Paul's secret for happiness, phone Colossians 3:12–17

With big opportunity/discovery, phone Isaiah 55

To get along with other people, phone Romans 12

Alternate Numbers:

For dealing with fear, call Psalm 47

For security, call Psalm 121:3

For assurance, call Mark 8:35

For reassurance, call Psalm 145:18

WHO ME? WORTHWHILE? YES, YOU!

All of These Numbers May Be Phoned Directly.

No Operator Assistance is Necessary.

All Lines to Heaven Are Available 24 Hours a Day.

Feed Your Faith, and Doubt Will Starve to Death.

PRAYER

Dear God,

May your blessing be upon all of us in our walk with You. Give us the deep desire to do whatever you have in store for us in spite of how fearful we might sometimes feel. Help us to know that you are our great guide in life. May we never cease to praise your name to all those we come in contact with by word or action. Thank you for being the great "I AM."

We love You,

Amen

"How do I love thee? Let me count the ways.
I love thee to the depth and breadth and height
My soul can reach..."
—Elizabeth Barrett Browning

"Those who love are but one step from heaven."
—James Russell Lowell

www.ingramcontent.com/pod-product-compliance
Lightning Source LLC
Chambersburg PA
CBHW070326100426
42743CB00011B/2576